SEDUCE MY MIND AND YOU CAN HAVE MY BODY

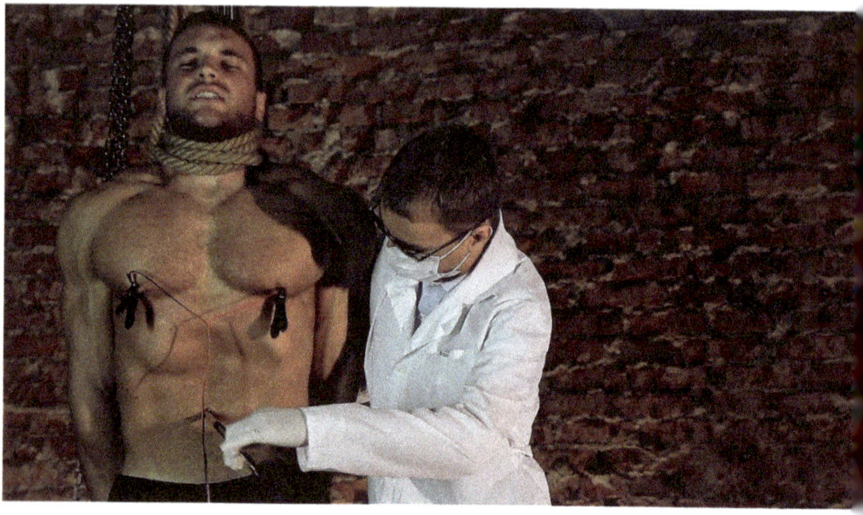

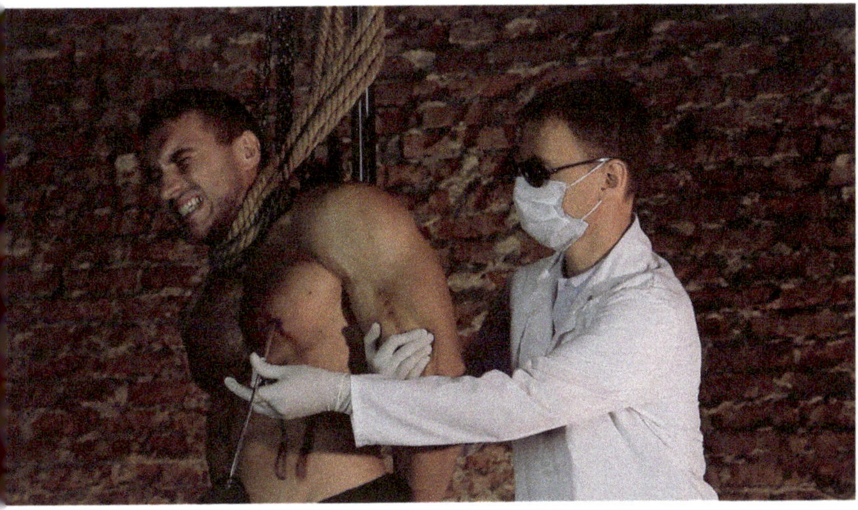

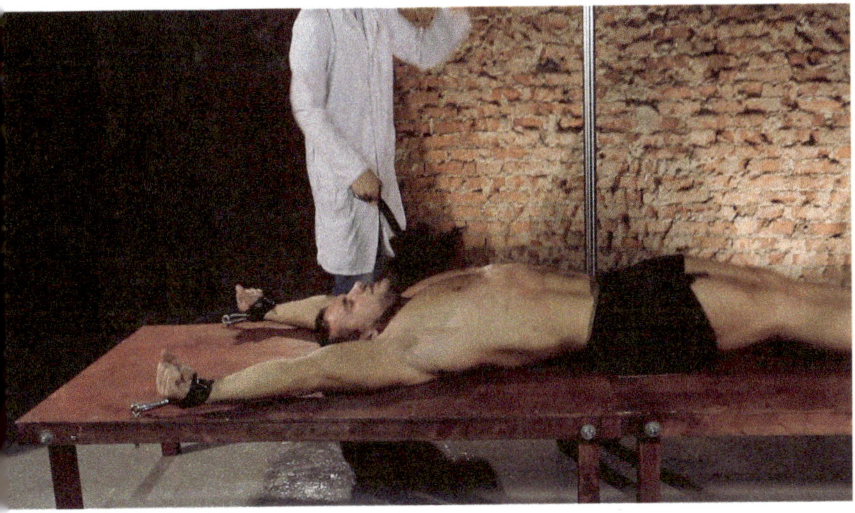

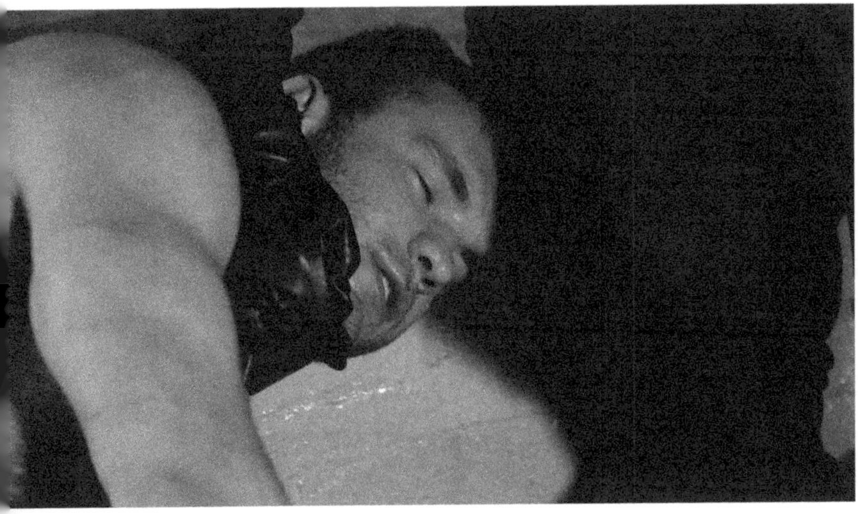

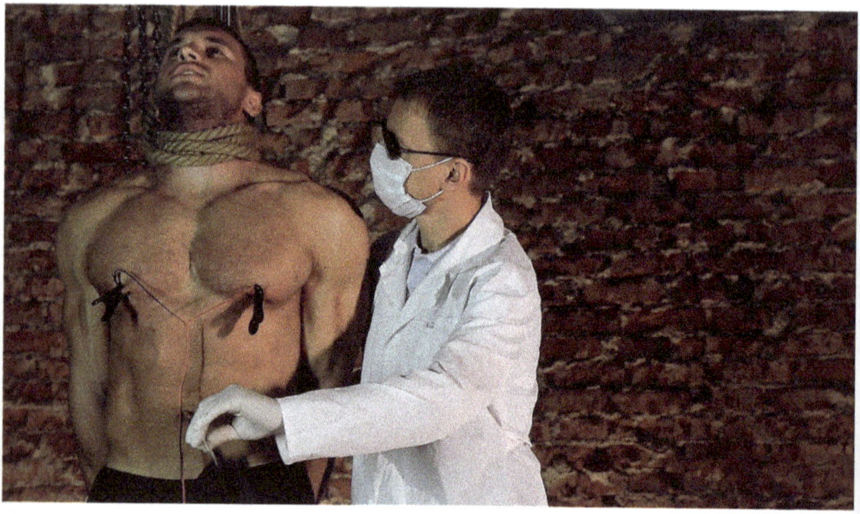

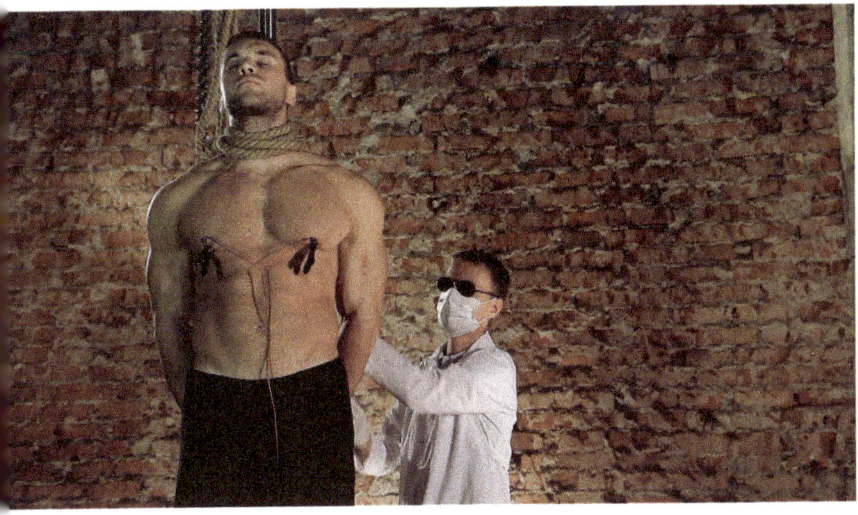

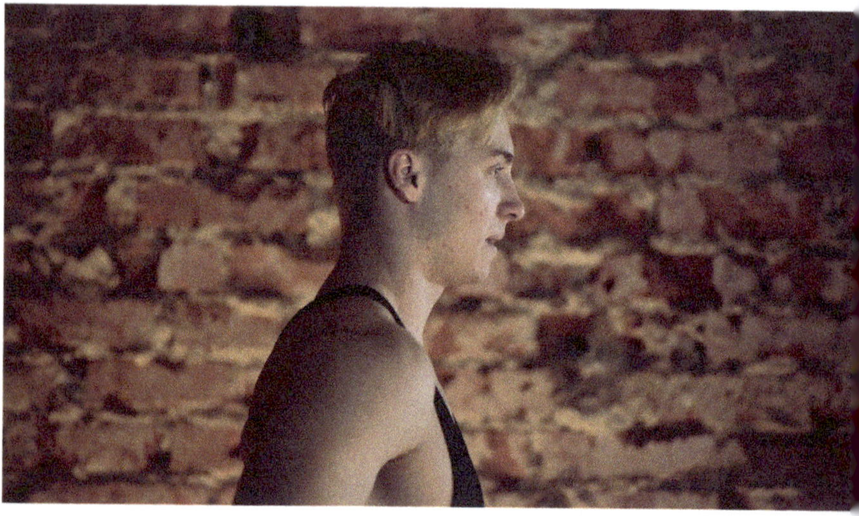

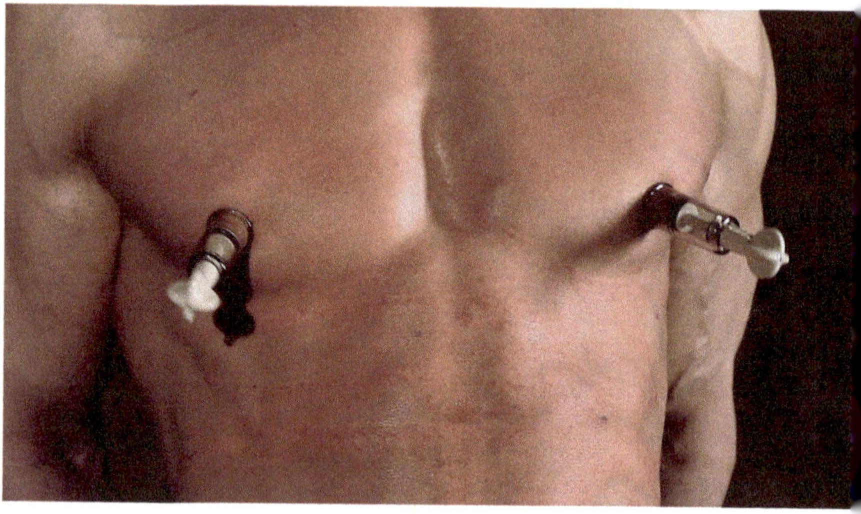

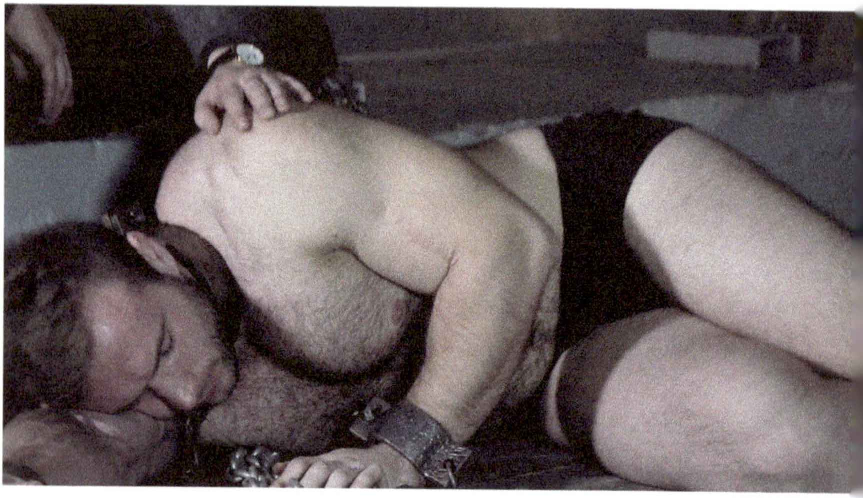

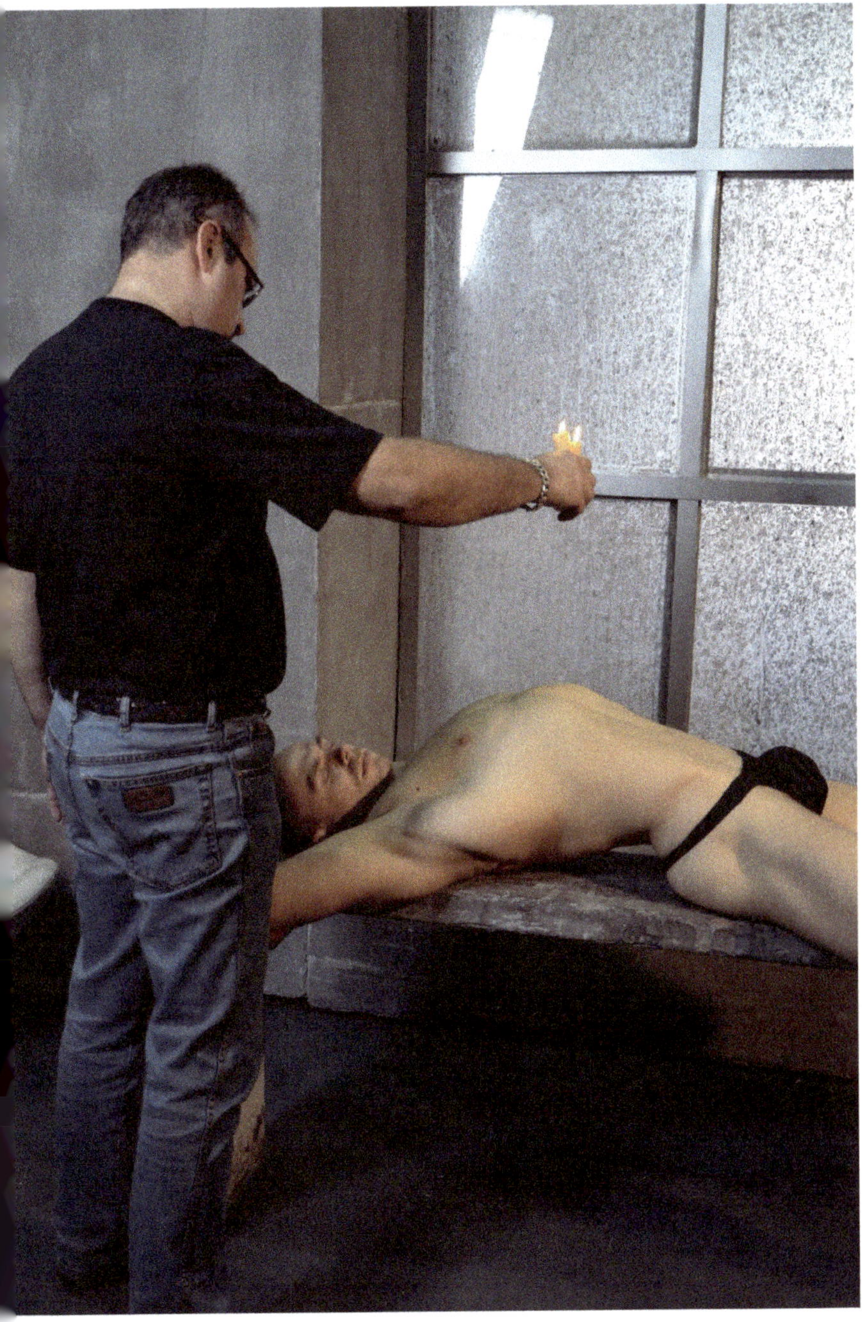

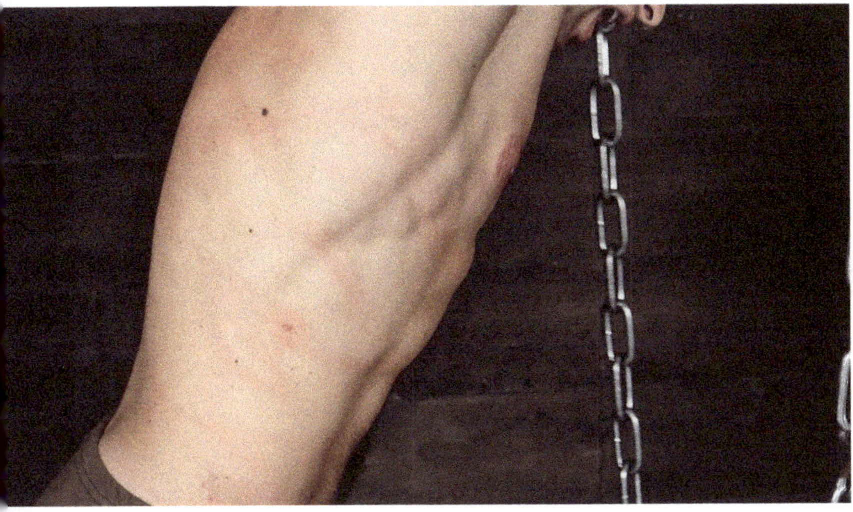

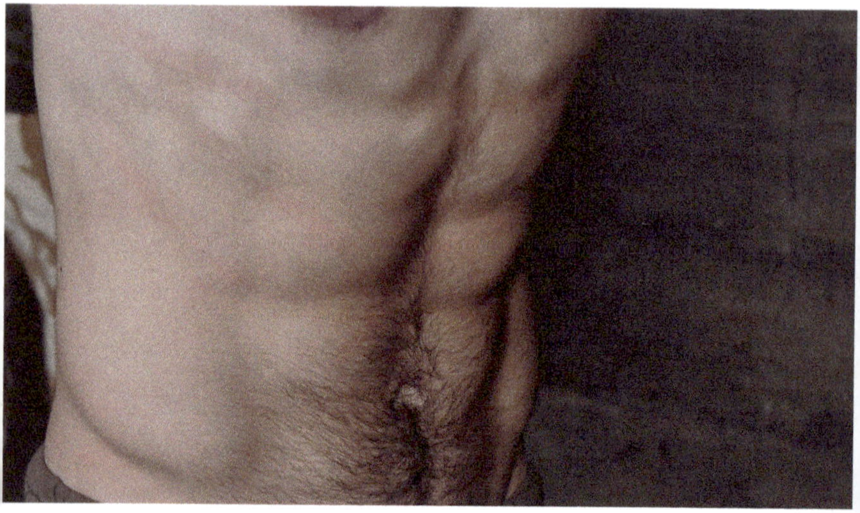

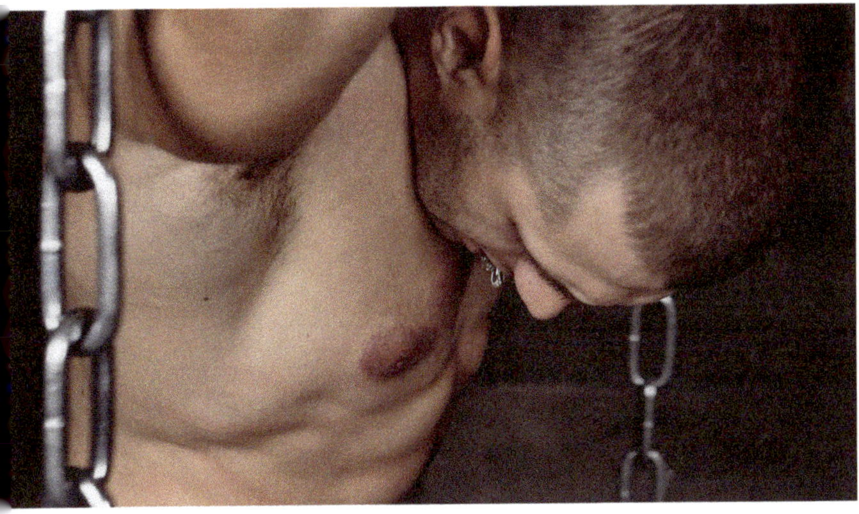

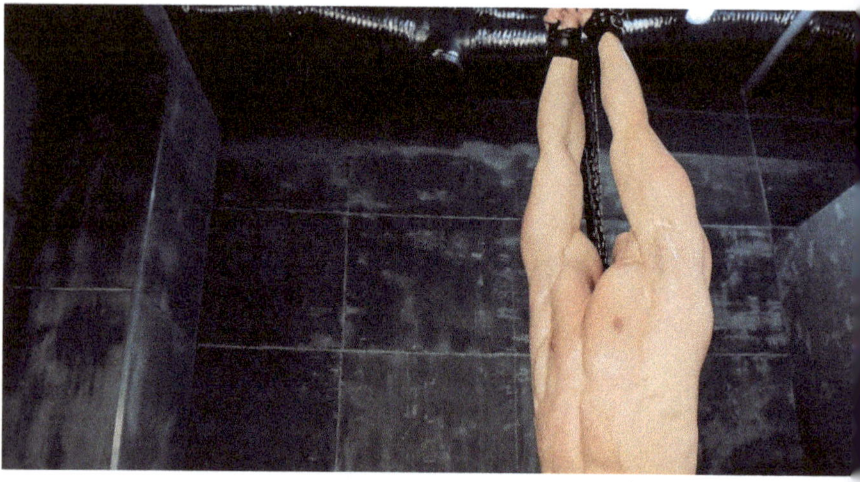

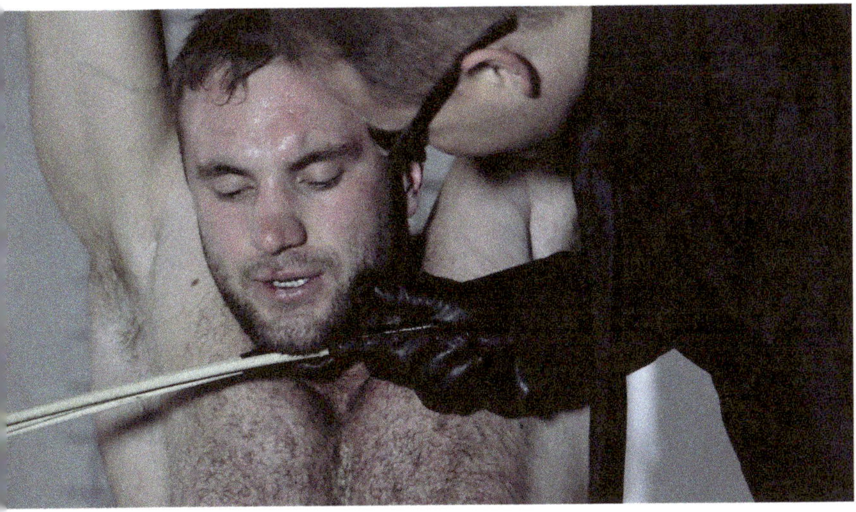

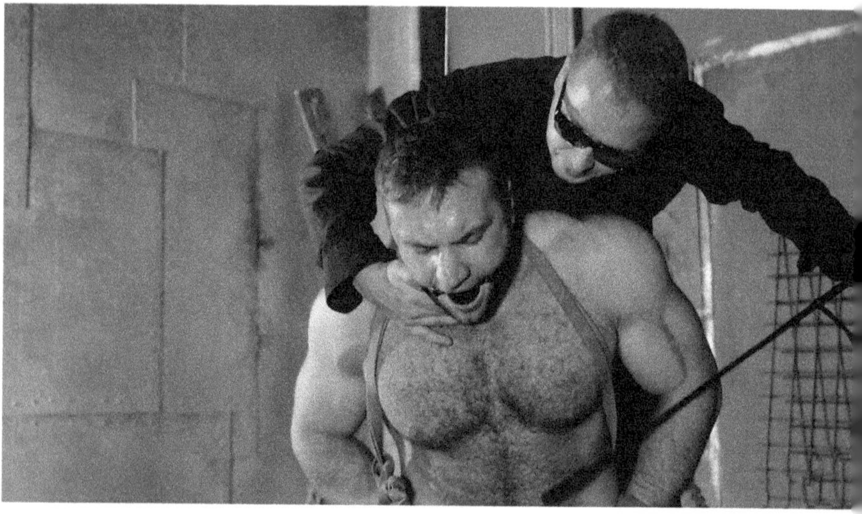

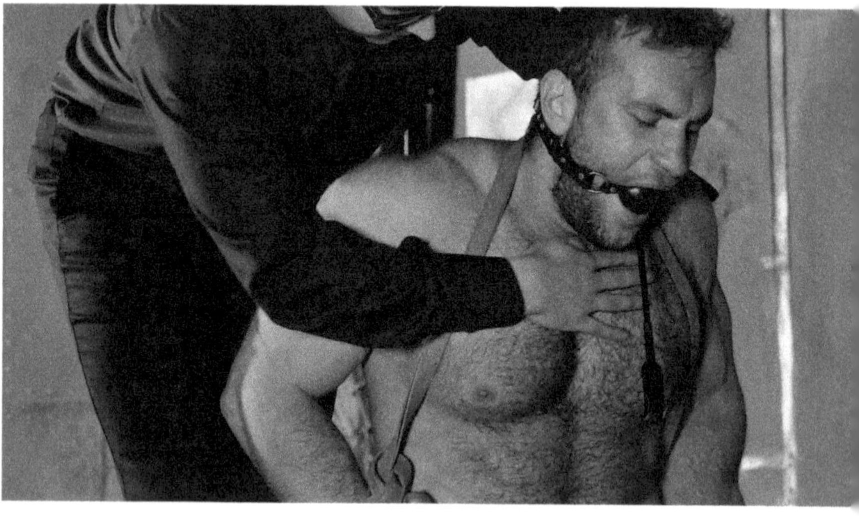

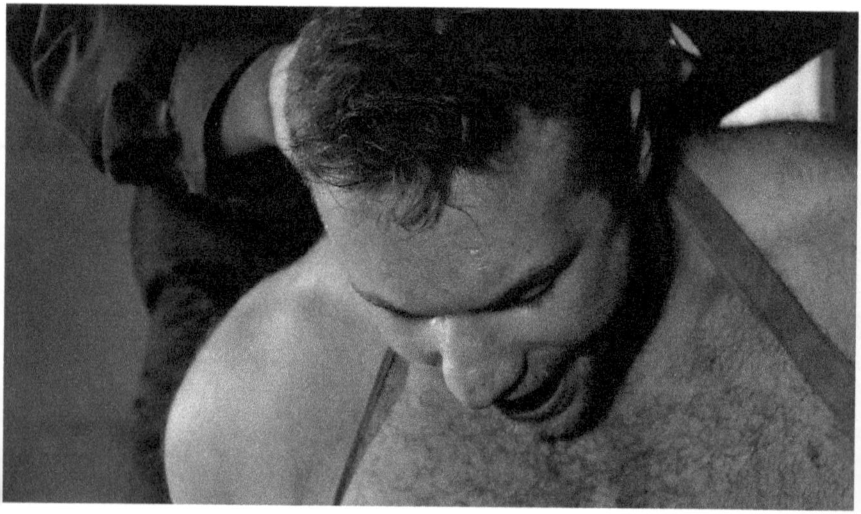

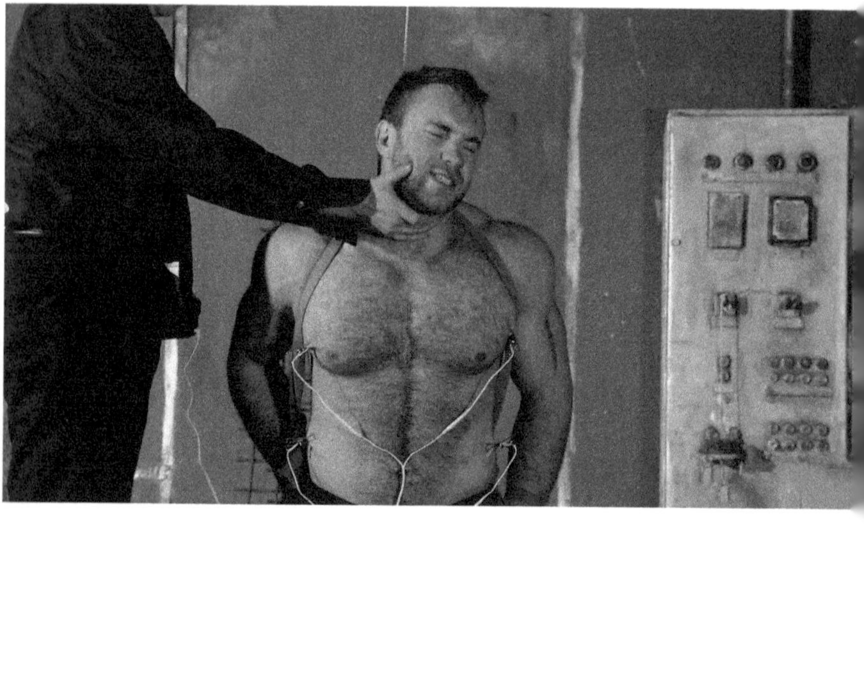

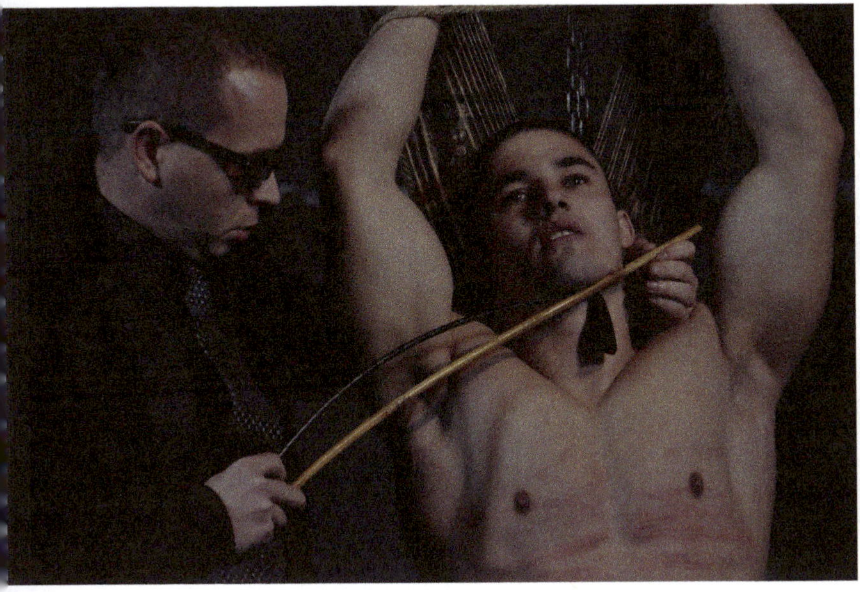

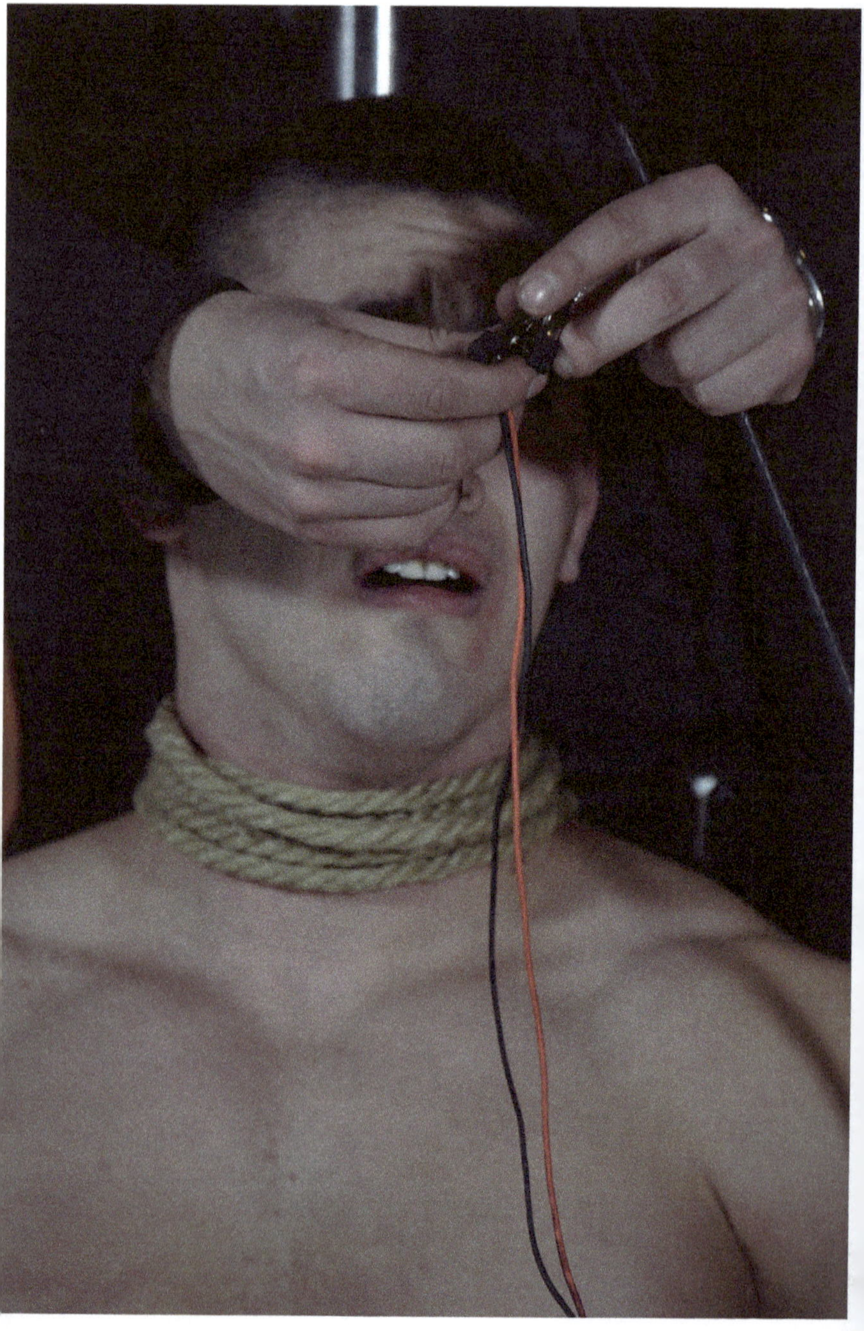

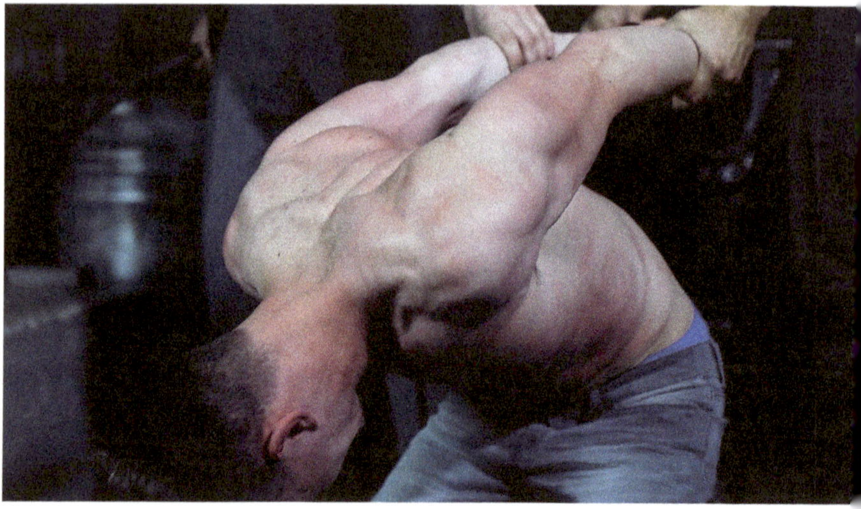

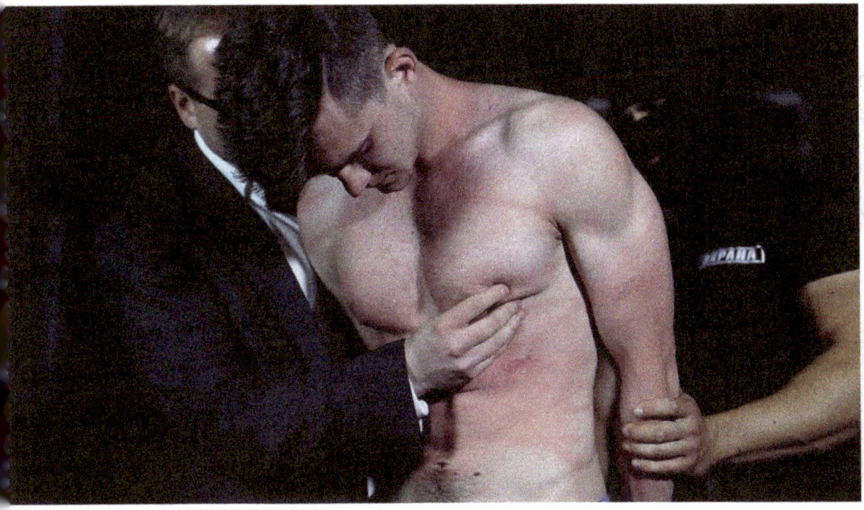

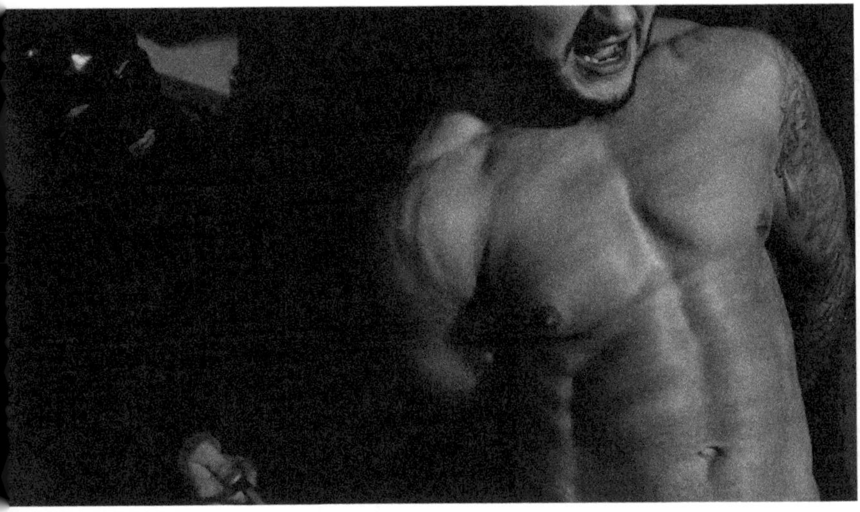

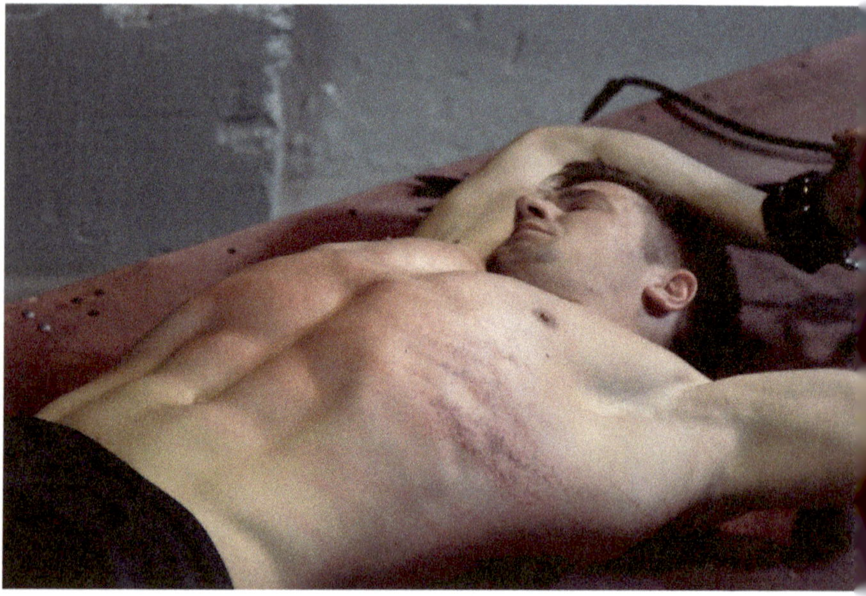

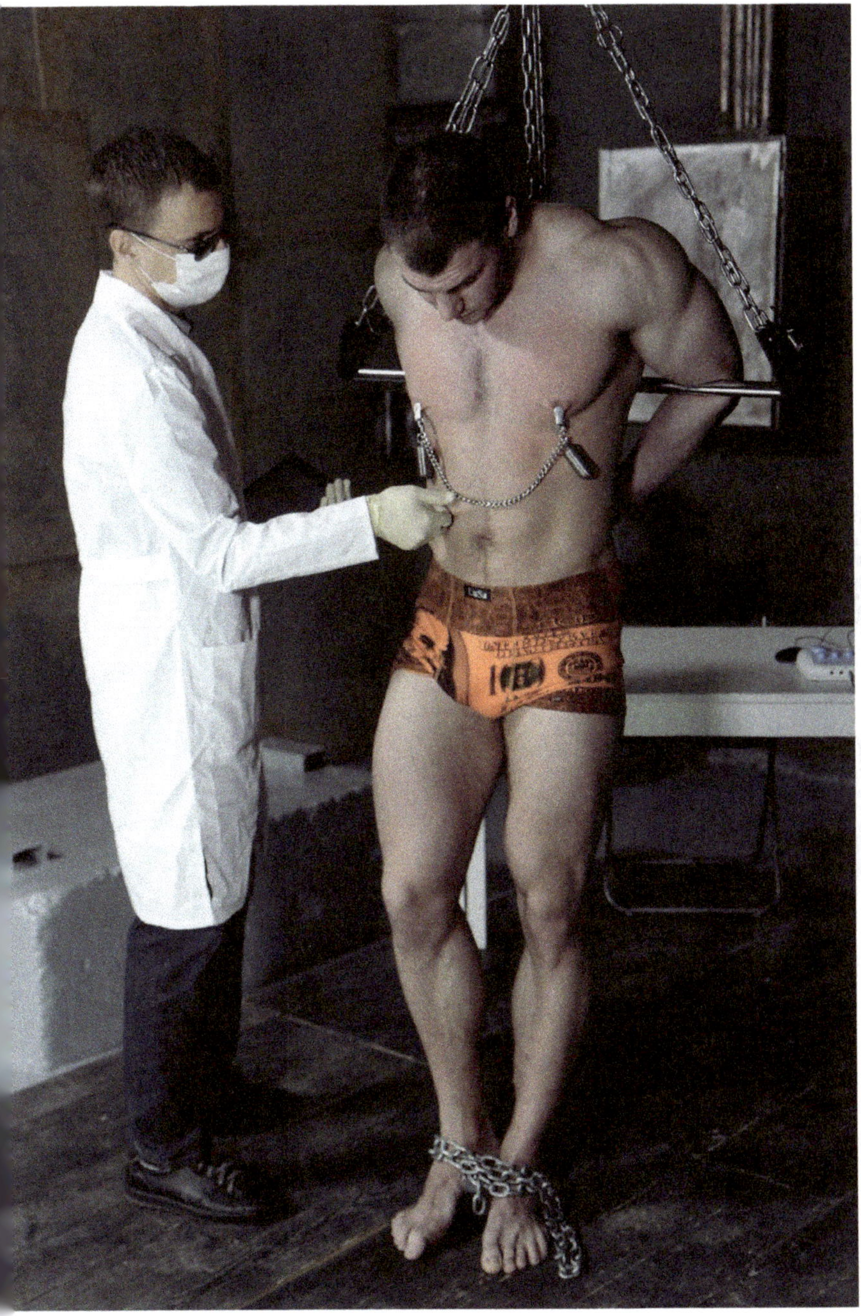

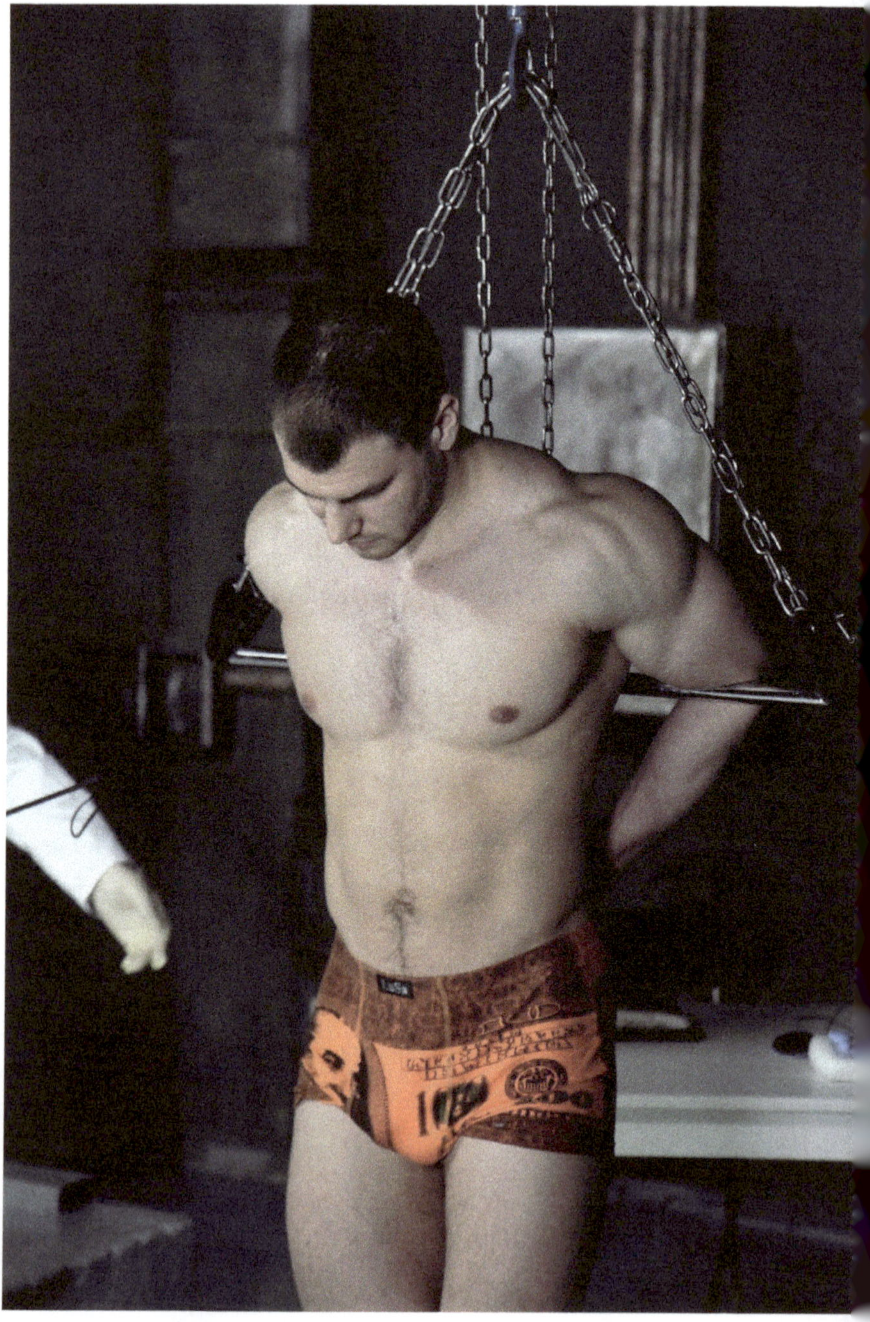

LuSa

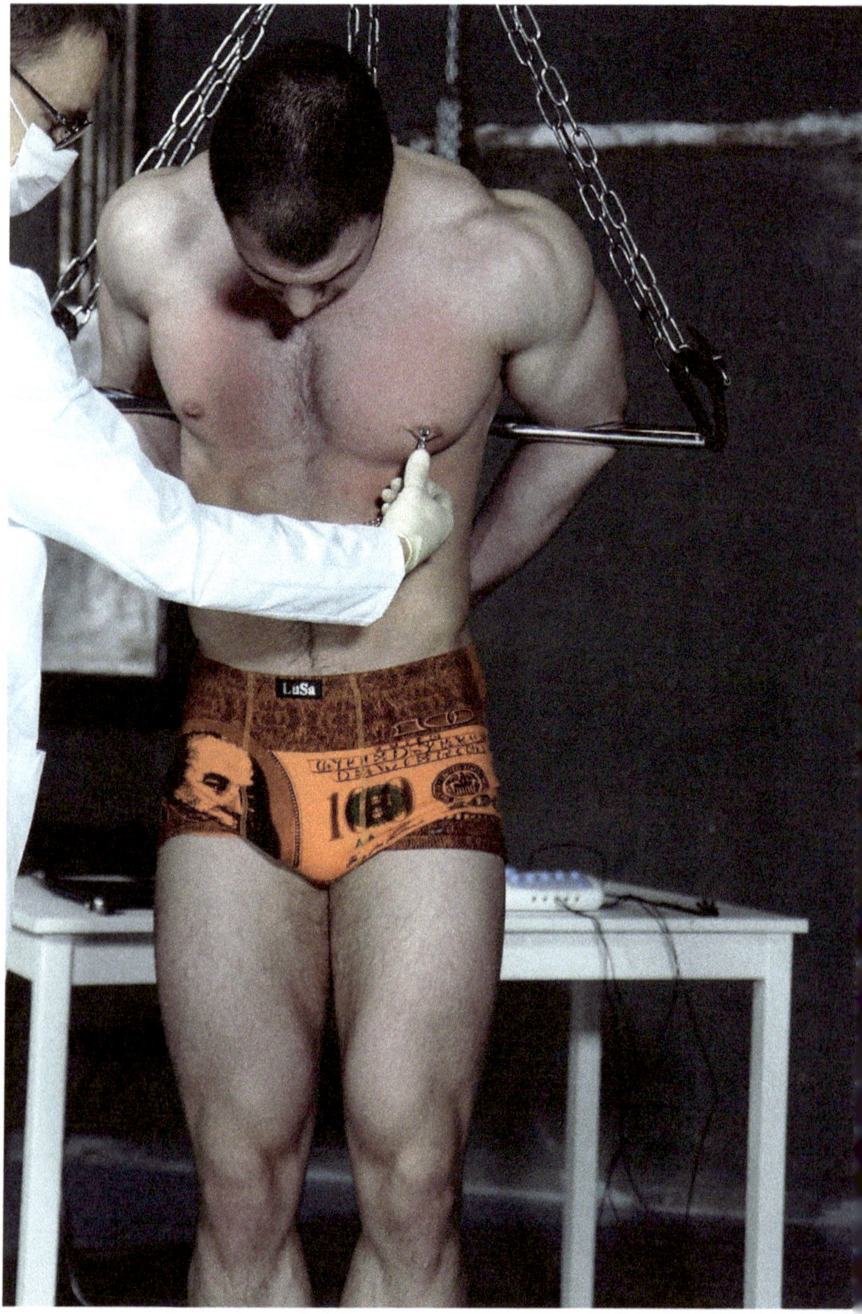
LuSa

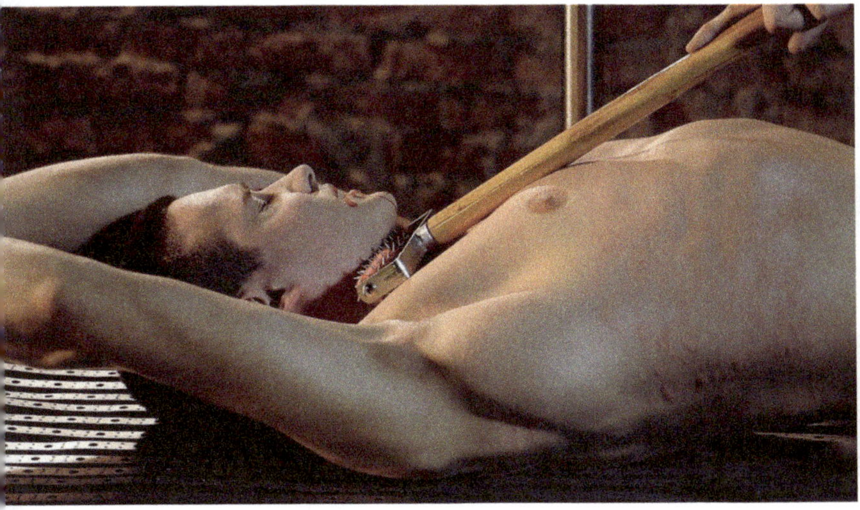

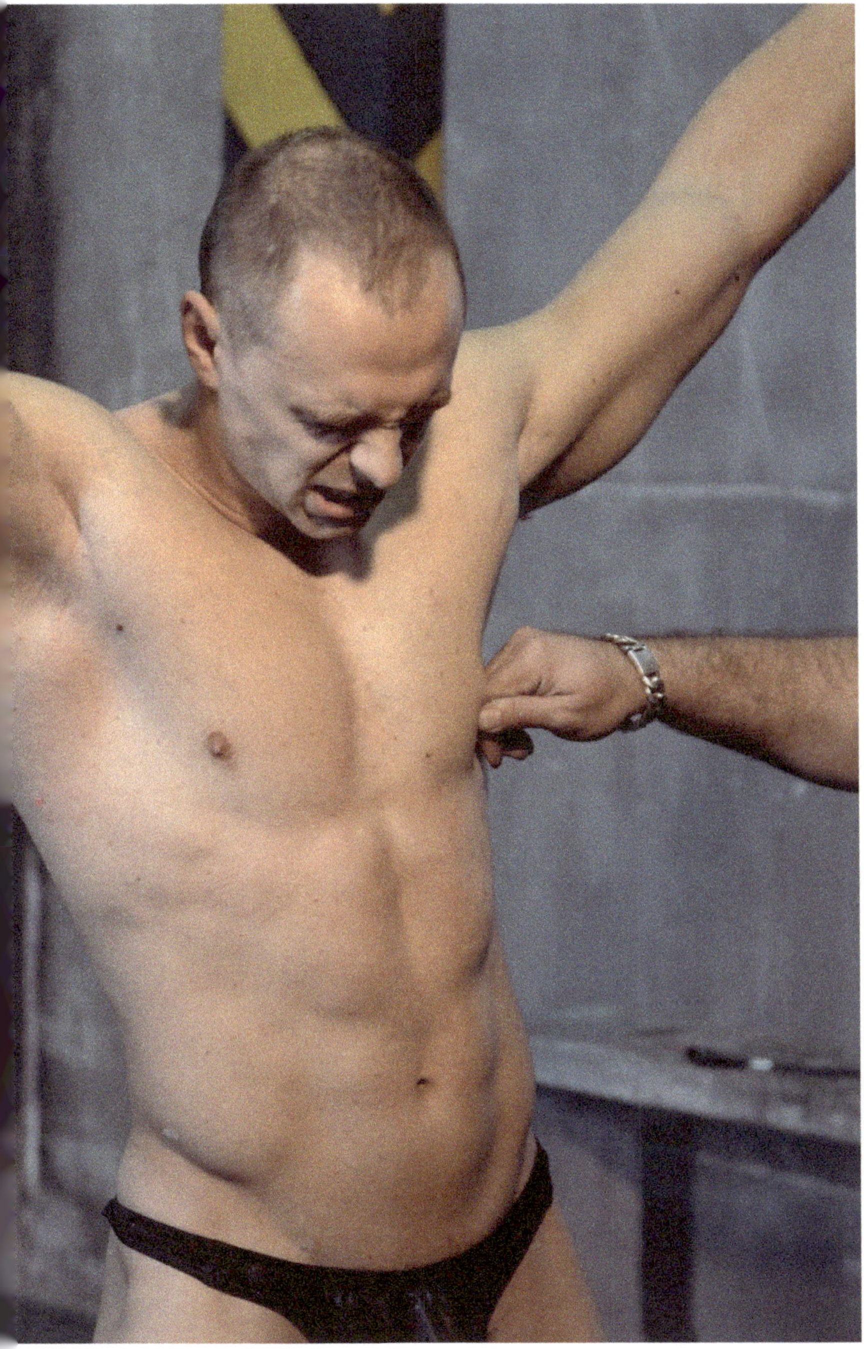

100

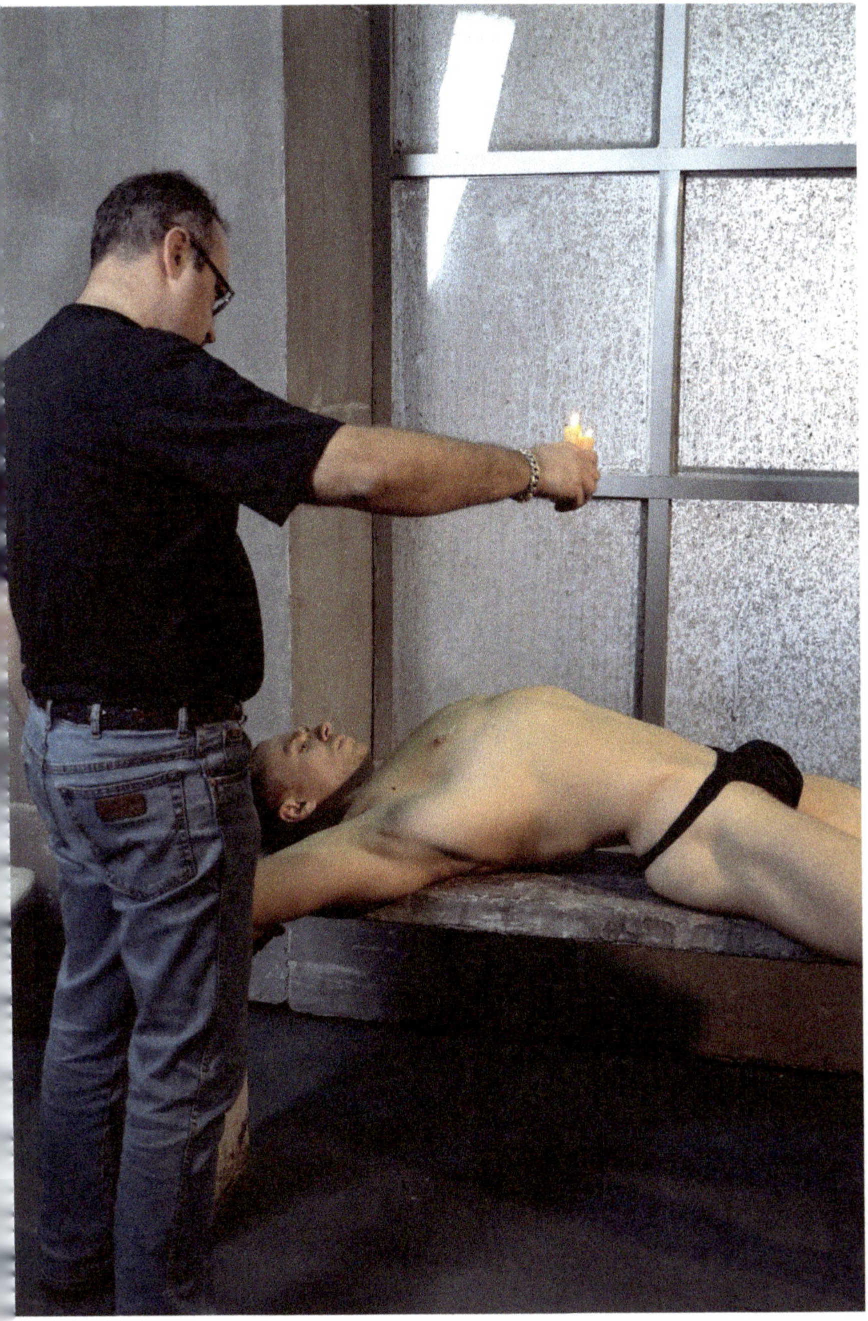

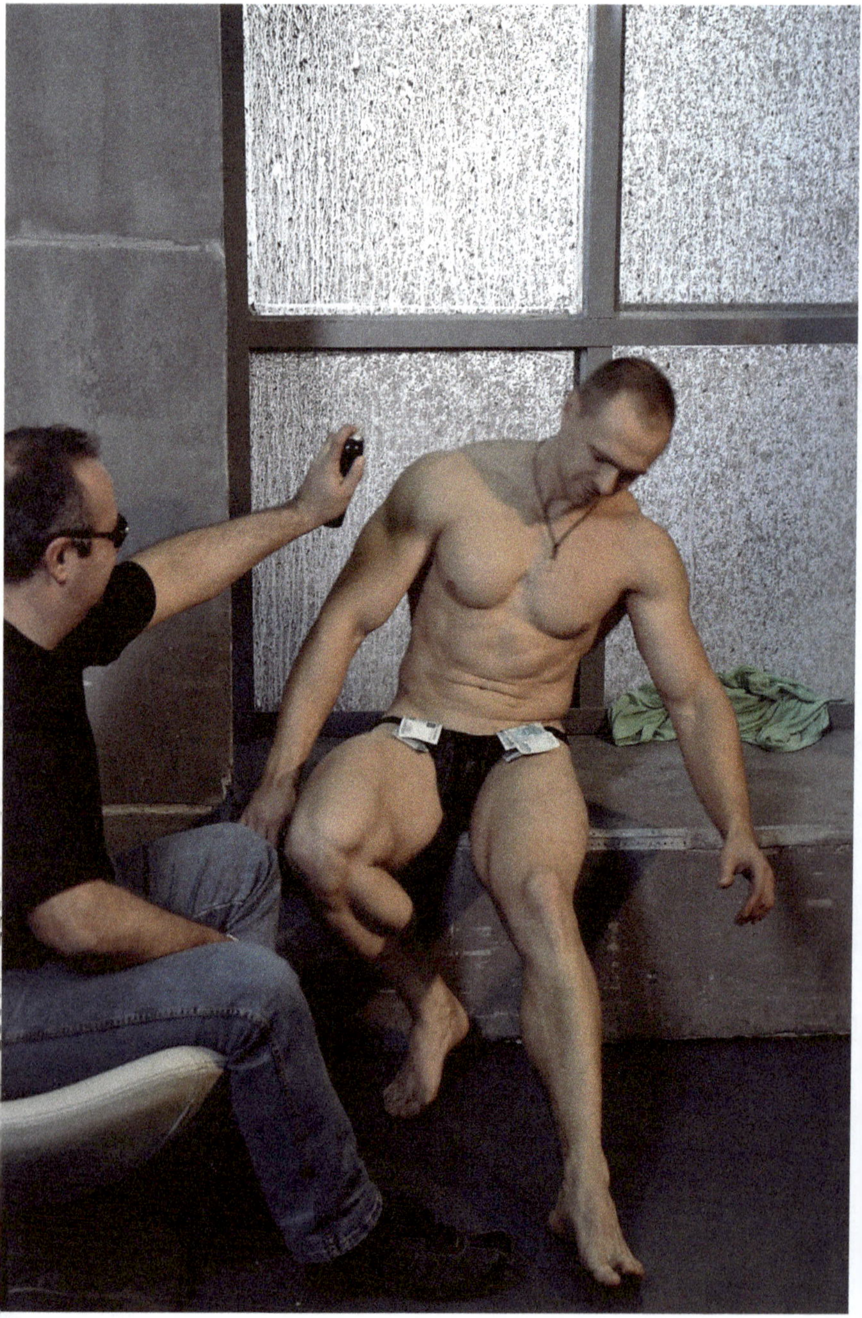

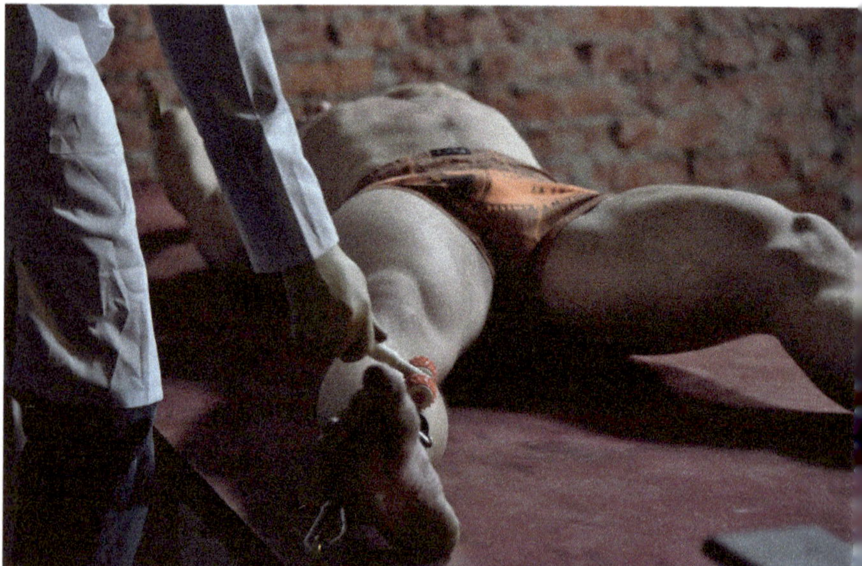

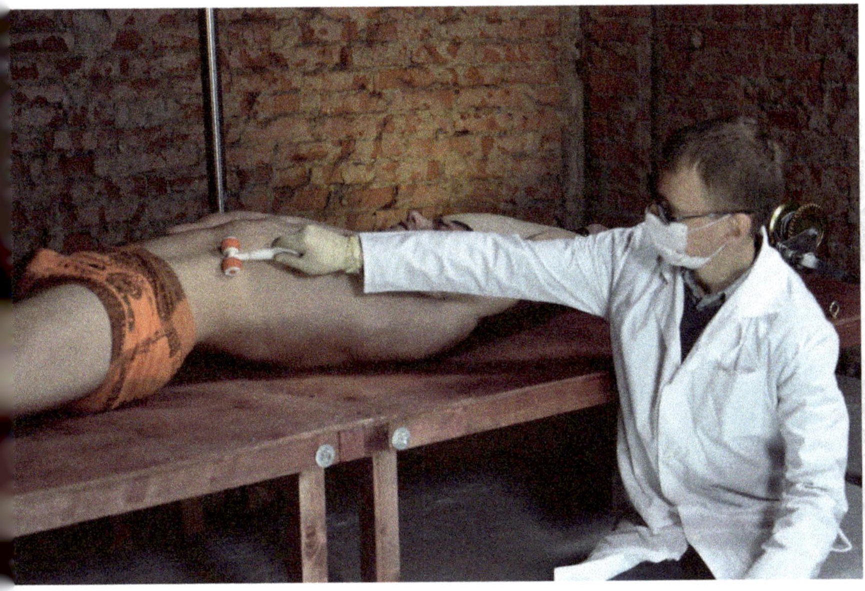

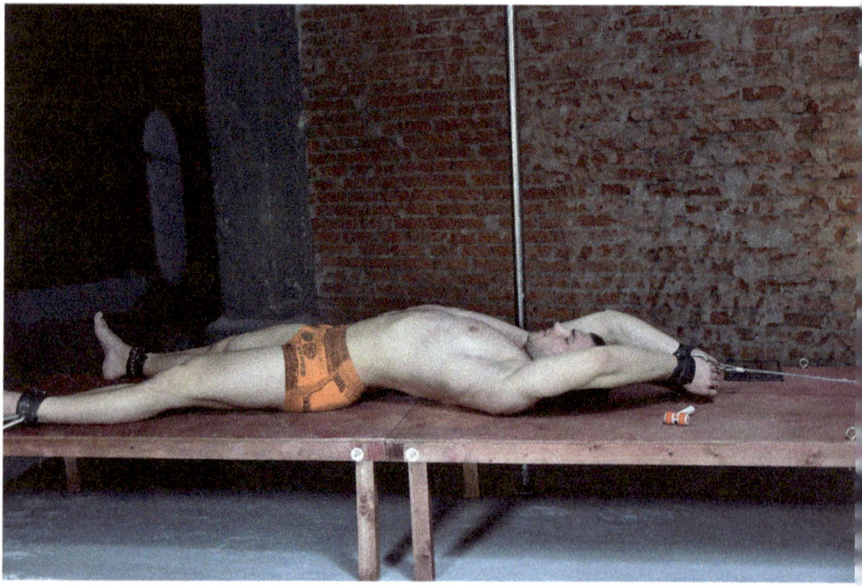

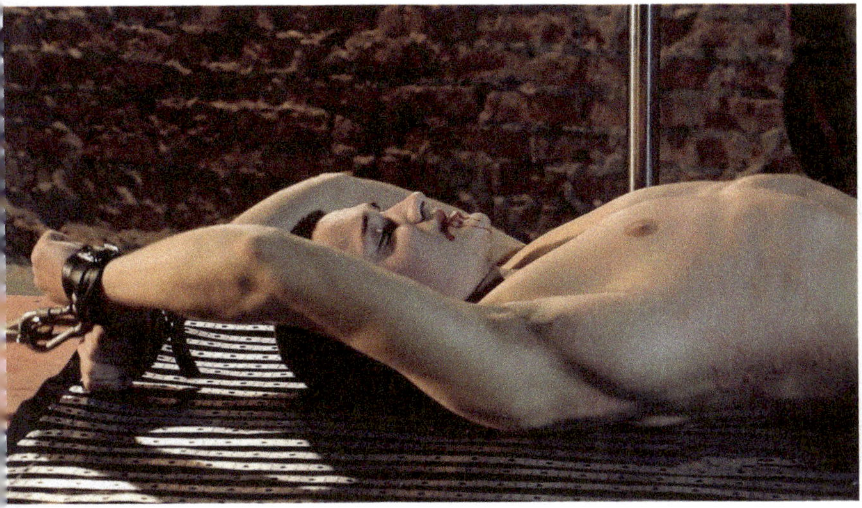

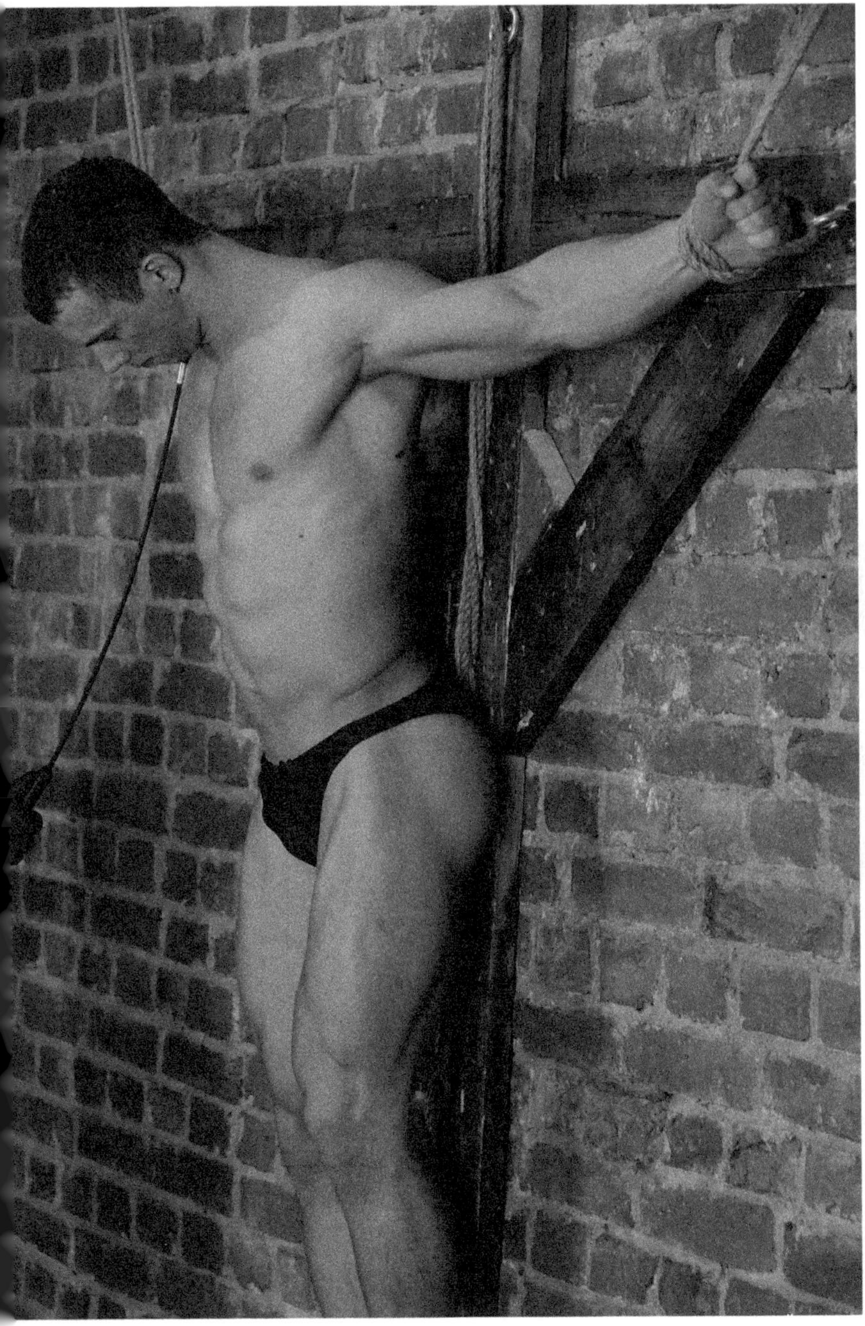

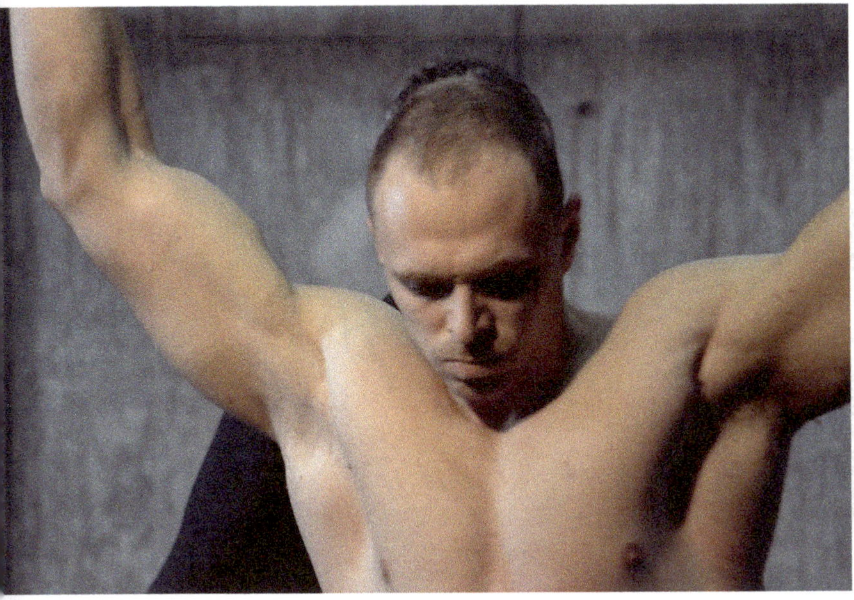

100

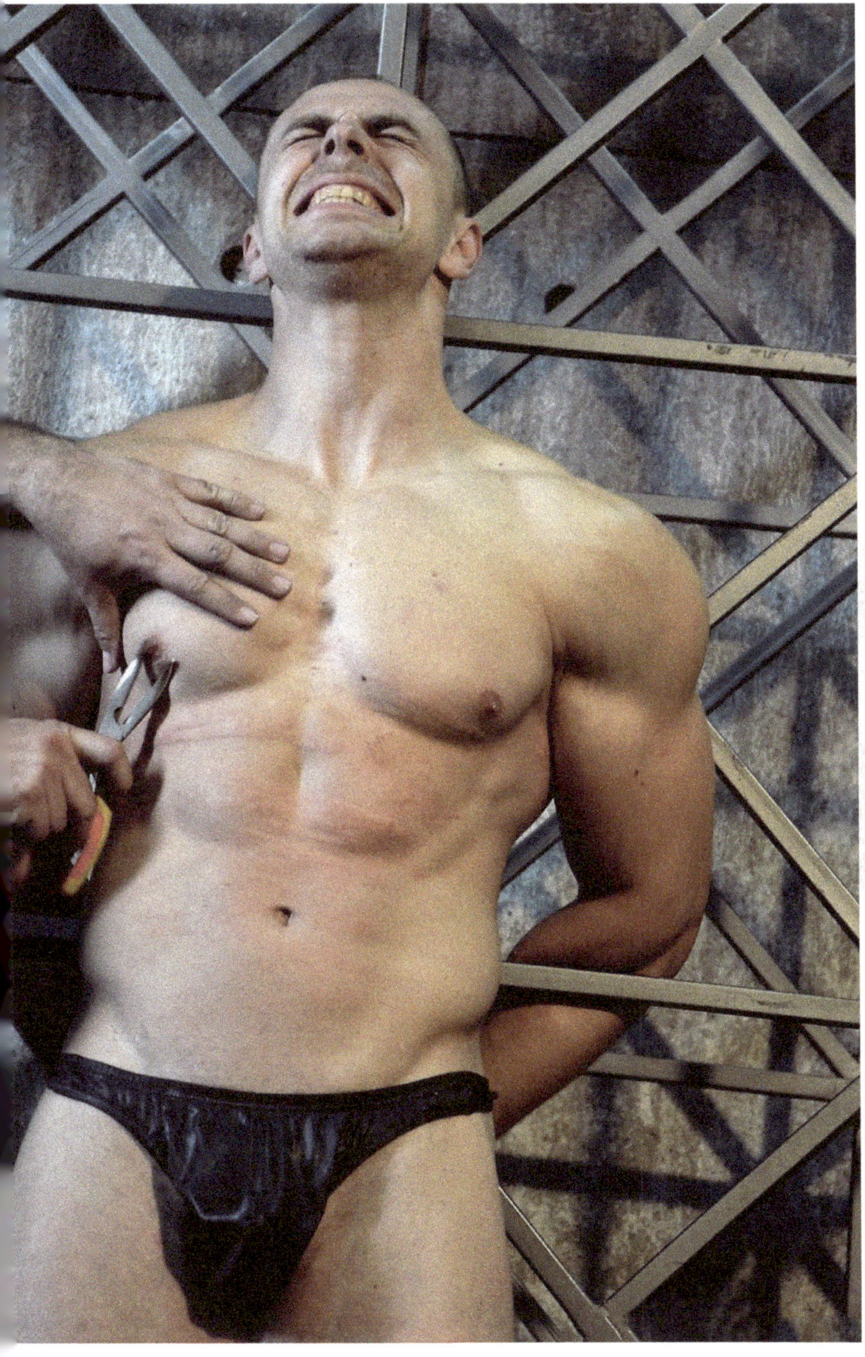

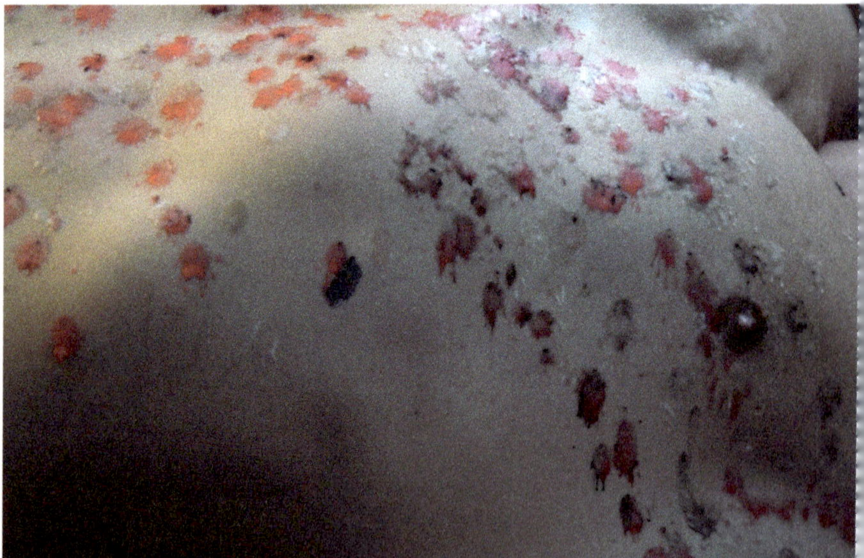

CPSIA information can be obtained
at www.ICGtesting.com
Printed in the USA
BVHW050816110319
542311BV00024B/1486/P

9 780368 379994